AF506222

The SUCCESSFUL MAN

A New Vision of Masculinity

COMPANION STUDY GUIDE

KENNETH G ALEXANDER

Desert Sky Press
Tucson, Arizona, USA

Copyright © 2026 Kenneth G Alexander

All rights reserved. This book may not be reproduced in whole or in part, stored in a retrieval system, or transmitted in any form or by any means electronic, mechanical, or other without written permission from the publisher, except by a reviewer, who may quote brief passages in a review.

Published by Desert Sky Press
Tucson, Arizona, USA
desertsky.press

Library of Congress Cataloging-in-Publication Data
Alexander, Kenneth G
The Successful Man: A New Vision of Masculinity – Companion Study Guide / Kenneth G Alexander

ISBN: 979-8-9908088-4-3 paperback

CONTENTS

INTRODUCTION

WHY THIS GUIDE EXISTS AND HOW IT HELPS

This guide was created to make the work in *The Successful Man* practical and usable.

The book explains the patterns. This guide helps you work with them in your own life so what you understand begins to show up in how you think, speak, and relate.

Each chapter helps you notice what is happening inside you, recognize your patterns, and see how you respond under pressure. That awareness creates space between what you feel and how you react.

From that space, you begin to make different choices.

Over time, those choices help you stay present in situations where you may have previously shut down, reacted, or disconnected. This is where change actually happens, not in big moments, but in how you handle what is right in front of you.

Most of what shaped us happened in relationship—families, teams, classrooms, locker rooms, and workplaces. Because of that, change often becomes clearer in relationship as well. While this guide can be used on your own, it becomes more effective when used with other men. Honest conversation reduces isolation and helps you see yourself more clearly.

The goal is not perfection. The goal is to stay present, respond with awareness, and live in a way that feels more grounded and connected.

WHO THIS GUIDE IS FOR

This guide is for anyone willing to look honestly at how they are living and how they are showing up.

It is for men who feel the pressure to hold everything together and are beginning to question the cost of that. It is for men who want to be more present in their relationships but do not always know how. It is for men learning how to recognize what they feel and express it more clearly.
It is also for leaders, partners, and facilitators who want to create space for this work.

You do not need the right language or a perfect starting point. What matters is your willingness to be honest and stay with yourself long enough to see what is there.

HOW TO USE THIS GUIDE

There is no single way to use this guide.

You can move through it alongside the book or return to sections based on what is happening in your life. Each chapter is designed to help you reflect, recognize where the material shows up, and apply it in a practical way.

If you are using it on your own, focus on honesty rather than completion. If you are using it in a group, keep the conversation grounded in real experience rather than theory.
Some sections will land right away. Others may take time. The value comes from returning to the work and staying with it.

USING THIS GUIDE IN A GROUP

This guide is designed to be used in conversation as well as on your own.

Most of what shaped us happened in relationship—families, teams, classrooms, locker rooms, and workplaces. Because of that, this work often becomes clearer and more meaningful when it is shared with others. Conversation reduces isolation and helps you see yourself more accurately.

A simple structure works best. Keep the focus on real experience rather than theory.

Suggested Flow (60–75 minutes):

1. **Check-in (10 minutes)**
   Each person shares how they are doing. Keep it honest and brief.
2. **What stood out (15 minutes)**
   Share what from the chapter or your reflections stayed with you.
3. **Where it shows up (20 minutes)**
   Talk about where this is showing up in your life right now.
4. **What you are working on (15 minutes)**
   Each person names one area they are focusing on this week.
5. **Close (5 minutes)**
   End with a simple check-out. No fixing or advising.

The goal is not to fix or advise each other. It is to speak honestly and listen without judgment.

Group Agreements:

- Speak from your own experience
- Listen without interrupting
- Do not offer advice unless asked
- Keep what is shared confidential

When the space is consistent and respectful, men begin to speak more openly and the sense of isolation begins to ease.

A SIMPLE PROMISE

This guide is here to support you, not to measure you.

There will be times when the work feels clear and times when it does not. What matters is your willingness to come back, stay present, and remain honest about your experience.

Over time, that consistency changes how you respond, how you relate, and how you live.

CHAPTER ONE

BEING A MAN—
HOW DID WE GET HERE?

SNAPSHOT

This chapter invites you to look at how your understanding of being a man was shaped.

- You were taught what a man "should" be long before you chose it
- Many of those expectations were inherited, not examined
- Emotional suppression was often presented as strength
- Performance and approval became tied to worth
- Disconnection from yourself often began early

Awareness is the first step toward choosing differently.

REFLECTION

Take your time with these. Answer honestly.

1. What did being a "real man" mean in the environment I grew up in?

2. Who taught me that, directly or indirectly?

3. What messages did I receive about how a man should act, feel, or respond?

4. When did I learn to hide, perform, or protect myself instead of being honest?

5. Where do I still feel pressure to "be a certain way" today?

____
____
____
____
____
____
____
____
____
____
____
____
____
____

AWARENESS

Where do you notice this showing up today?

☐ In conversations where I avoid saying what I really feel
☐ In work situations where I perform instead of being honest
☐ In relationships where I shut down or withdraw
☐ When I feel pressure to appear strong or in control
☐ When I avoid vulnerability or discomfort
☐ Other: _______________________________

What does that look like for you?

____
____
____
____
____
____
____
____
____

PRACTICE

<u>When You Notice...</u>	<u>Try This</u>
Emotional shutdown	➤ Bring your attention to your chest and notice what is there without pushing it away
Performing instead of being yourself	➤ Pause and ask: "What is actually true for me right now?"
Feeling disconnected from yourself	➤ Take 3 slow breaths and let your body settle
Pressure to appear strong or in control	➤ Name what you are actually feeling instead of overriding it

THIS WEEK

Choose one area where you want to show up differently.

This week, I will:

One moment I will practice this in:

What support do I need to follow through?

RESET

Use this anytime you feel off, overwhelmed, or disconnected:

- Pause
- Take a slow breath
- Bring your attention back into your body
- Ask: "What am I actually feeling?"
- Stay with it before reacting

WEEKLY REFLECTION

Come back to this after a few days.

What did I notice this week?

____
____
____
____
____
____
____
____
____
____
____
____

Where did I show up differently?

____
____
____
____
____
____
____
____
____
____
____

Where did I fall back into old patterns?

____
____
____
____
____
____
____
____
____
____

What did I learn about myself?

____
____
____
____
____
____
____
____
____
____
____

Where did I fall back into old patterns?

CHAPTER TWO

FOUNDATIONAL OVERVIEW

SNAPSHOT

This chapter establishes the language and concepts used throughout the book.

- Many ideas about masculinity were inherited, not chosen
- Male is biological, but identity is shaped through experience
- Masculine and feminine are energies present in everyone
- The Doctrine reshaped masculinity into performance and pressure
- External validation and fear-based motivation influence behavior
- Emotional suppression leads to disconnection
- The heart is a source of clarity and stability
- Grounding and breath help you return to yourself

REFLECTION

Take your time with these. Answer honestly.

1. What definitions of masculinity have I been living by?

2. Which of those feel true to me, and which feel inherited or expected?

3. How do I understand masculine and feminine energy in my own life?

4. Where do I look for approval or validation to feel like I am enough?

5. How do I typically respond to my emotions—do I allow them or suppress them?

____

____

____

____

____

____

____

____

____

____

____

____

____

____

AWARENESS

Where do you notice this showing up today?

☐ In how I define success

☐ In how I respond under pressure

☐ In how I handle emotions

☐ In how I relate to others

☐ In how I measure my worth

☐ Other: ____

What does that look like for you?

____

____

____

____

____

____
____
____
____
____
____
____
____
____
____

PRACTICE

When You Notice...	Try This
Pressure to perform or prove yourself	➢ Ask: "Is this coming from me or from what I was taught?"
Emotional shutdown or numbness	➢ Name what you are feeling without trying to fix it
Seeking approval or validation	➢ Bring your attention back to what you believe is true
Feeling overwhelmed or stressed	➢ Slow your breathing and let your body settle

THIS WEEK

Choose one area where you want to show up differently.

This week, I will:

____
____
____
____
____
____

One moment I will practice this in:

What support do I need to follow through?

RESET

Use this anytime you feel off, overwhelmed, or disconnected:

- Pause
- Take a slow breath
- Bring your attention back into your body
- Ask: "What am I actually feeling?"
- Stay with it before reacting

WEEKLY REFLECTION

Come back to this after a few days.

What did I notice this week?

____
____
____
____
____
____
____
____
____
____
____
____

Where did I show up differently?

____
____
____
____
____
____
____
____
____
____
____

Where did I fall back into old patterns?

What did I learn about myself?

CHAPTER THREE

COMPETITION

SNAPSHOT

This chapter invites you to look at how competition shaped your identity and how it may still be influencing how you relate to others.

- Competition was often introduced early as a way to measure worth
- Winning became associated with being valued or respected
- Losing could feel like failure, not just an outcome
- Comparison replaced connection in many environments
- Success became something to prove instead of something to experience
- You can choose connection without losing your drive

REFLECTION

Take your time with these. Answer honestly.

1. What did competition look like in my childhood (sports, school, family, friendships)?

2. When did I start connecting winning with my value or identity?

3. How did I feel when I lost, compared to when I won?

4. Where in my life do I still compare myself to others?

5. What would it look like to experience success without needing to compete?

____

____

____

____

____

____

____

____

____

____

____

____

____

____

____

____

____

AWARENESS

Where do you notice this showing up today?

☐ Comparing myself to others in work or life
☐ Feeling like I need to win to feel good about myself
☐ Struggling to celebrate others' success
☐ Turning situations into competition unnecessarily
☐ Feeling tension or pressure around performance
☐ Other: _______________________________________

What does that look like for you?

____

____

____

____

____
____
____
____
____
____
____
____
____
____
____
____
____

PRACTICE

<u>When You Notice...</u>	<u>Try This</u>
Comparing yourself to others	➤ Bring your attention back to yourself and ask: "What matters to me right now?"
Performing instead of being yourself	➤ Pause and ask: What would connection look like here?"
Tension around performance	➤ Take a slow breath and return to the present moment
Turning everything into competition	➤ Notice the impulse and choose curiosity instead of comparison

THIS WEEK

Choose one area where you want to show up differently.

This week, I will:

____
____
____
____

One moment I will practice this in:

What support do I need to follow through?

RESET

- Use this anytime you feel pressure, comparison, or tension:
- Pause
- Take a slow breath
- Bring your attention back to yourself
- Ask: "What actually matters right now?"
- Choose connection over comparison

WEEKLY REFLECTION

Come back to this after a few days.

What did I notice this week?

____
____
____
____
____
____
____
____
____
____
____
____
____
____

Where did I show up differently?

____
____
____
____
____
____
____
____
____
____
____

Where did I fall back into old patterns?

What did I learn about myself?

CHAPTER FOUR

ACHIEVEMENT

SNAPSHOT

**This chapter invites you to look at how achievement became
tied to your sense of worth.**

- You were often rewarded for what you did, not for who
  you are
- Productivity became a measure of value
- Rest could feel uncomfortable and like falling behind
- Achievement created pressure instead of fulfillment
- External success did not always match how you felt
  internally
- You can choose alignment over constant striving

REFLECTION

Take your time with these. Answer honestly.

1. What messages did I receive about success and achievement growing up?

____

2. When did I begin to connect my worth to what I accomplish?

____

3. How do I feel when I am not being productive?

4. Where in my life am I pushing even when I feel exhausted?

5. What would it look like to measure my life differently?

____

____

____

____

____

____

____

____

____

____

____

____

AWARENESS

Where do you notice this showing up today?

- ☐ Overworking or pushing past exhaustion
- ☐ Feeling like I am never doing enough
- ☐ Difficulty resting without guilt
- ☐ Tying my mood to productivity
- ☐ Constant pressure to achieve or prove myself
- ☐ Other: ____

What does that look like for you?

____

____

____

____

____

____

____

PRACTICE

When You Notice...	**Try This**
Overworking or pushing past your limit	➤ Pause and take a slow breath before continuing
Feeling like you are not doing enough	➤ Acknowledge what you have already done today
Difficulty resting	➤ Allow yourself a moment without needing to earn it
Pressure to achieve or prove yourself	➤ Ask: "Is this aligned with me or driven by pressure?"

THIS WEEK

Choose one area where you want to show up differently.

This week, I will:

One moment I will practice this in:

What support do I need to follow through?

RESET

- Use this anytime you feel pressure, urgency, or exhaustion:
- Pause
- Take a slow breath
- Bring your attention back into your body
- Ask: "Am I pushing or am I aligned?"
- Choose one small, honest step

WEEKLY REFLECTION

Come back to this after a few days.

What did I notice this week?

____
____
____
____
____
____
____
____
____
____
____

Where did I show up differently?

____
____
____
____
____
____
____
____
____
____
____

Where did I fall back into old patterns?

What did I learn about myself?

CHAPTER FIVE

VALIDATION

SNAPSHOT

**This chapter invites you to look at how the need to be liked
shaped how you show up in the world.**

- Approval was often tied to safety and acceptance
- You may adjust yourself to avoid rejection or conflict
- Saying what others wanted to hear became a habit
- Discomfort was often avoided to maintain connection
- Your sense of worth can depend on how others respond to you
- Your truth may have been set aside to keep the peace
- You can choose honesty without losing connection

REFLECTION

Take your time with these. Answer honestly.

1. Where do I look for approval and validation in my life?

2. When do I notice myself changing or adjusting to be accepted?

3. Where do I tend to say yes when I really mean no?

4. What am I afraid might happen if I am fully honest?

5. What would it feel like to show up without needing approval?

____

____

____

____

____

____

____

____

____

____

____

____

____

AWARENESS

Where do you notice this showing up today?

- ☐ Saying yes when I want to say no
- ☐ Avoiding difficult conversations
- ☐ Holding back what I really think or feel
- ☐ Adjusting myself depending on who I am with
- ☐ Feeling anxious about how others see me
- ☐ Other:

____

What does that look like for you?

____

____

____

____

PRACTICE

When You Notice...	**Try This**
People-pleasing	➢ Pause and ask: "What is true for me right now?"
Avoiding honesty	➢ Take a breath and say one thing that is real, even if it is small
Saying yes when you mean no	➢ Give yourself a moment before responding
Fear of disapproval	➢ Stay with the feeling instead of adjusting yourself immediately

THIS WEEK

Choose one area where you want to show up differently.

This week, I will:

One moment I will practice this in:

What support do I need to follow through?

RESET

- Use this anytime you feel pressure to please or perform:
- Pause
- Take a slow breath
- Bring your attention back to yourself
- Ask: "What is true for me right now?"
- Respond from that place

WEEKLY REFLECTION

Come back to this after a few days.

What did I notice this week?

Where did I show up differently?

Where did I fall back into old patterns?

What did I learn about myself?

CHAPTER SIX

CHASING

SNAPSHOT

**This chapter invites you to look at how the pursuit of money and
wealth has shaped how you define success and how you show
up in your life.**

- Money becomes tied to identity, status, and security
- Success is measured by accumulation rather than
  alignment
- You may feel pressure to earn, prove, and provide
  constantly
- The pursuit of more can override presence and
  connection
- Enough can feel like it's always just out of reach
- You may sacrifice relationships, joy, or health in the
  process
- Chasing can become a cycle that never feels complete
- Awareness allows you to step off the treadmill and
  redefine your relationship with money and success

REFLECTION

Take your time with these. Answer honestly.

1. What am I chasing right now?

2. When do I feel like I need more to be satisfied?

3. What do I believe will change once I get what I am chasing?

4. Where do I feel pressure to earn, prove, or provide even when I am tired?

5. What would it feel like to have enough and be present with what I already have?

AWARENESS

Where do you notice this showing up today?

☐ Measuring my worth by income, success, or status
☐ Feeling like I am behind financially or professionally
☐ Difficulty slowing down or stepping away from work
☐ Restlessness even when I have achieved something meaningful
☐ Believing more money or success will finally make me feel secure
☐ Other: ____

What does that look like for you?

____
____
____
____
____
____
____
____
____
____
____
____
____
____
____

PRACTICE

When You Notice...	Try This
Constant chasing or striving for more	➢ Pause and notice what is already here
Feeling like you need more money or success	➢ Ask: "What is enough right now?"
Pressure to earn, prove, or provide	➢ Take a breath and check in with how you feel
Looking ahead instead of being present	➢ Bring your attention back to this moment

THIS WEEK

Choose one area where you want to show up differently.

This week, I will:

____
____
____
____
____
____
____
____
____
____

One moment I will practice this in:

____
____
____
____
____
____
____
____
____
____

What support do I need to follow through?

____
____
____
____
____
____
____
____

RESET

- Use this anytime you feel pressure to please or perform:
- Pause
- Take a slow breath
- Bring your attention back to yourself
- Ask: "What is true for me right now?"
- Respond from that place

WEEKLY REFLECTION

Come back to this after a few days.

What did I notice this week?

Where did I show up differently?

Where did I fall back into old patterns?

What did I learn about myself?

Where did I fall back into old patterns?

CHAPTER SEVEN

FREEDOM

SNAPSHOT

This chapter invites you to explore what true freedom looks like beyond the constant pursuit of money and achievement.

- Freedom is often postponed for a future version of success
- You may feel stuck in cycles of earning and proving
- Financial goals can become emotional pressure
- The belief that "more is needed" can quietly drive your decisions
- You may struggle to slow down or step away
- Time, presence, and choice are often sacrificed in the process
- Enough can feel unfamiliar or even uncomfortable
- Awareness allows you to move from chasing to choosing how you live

REFLECTION

Take your time with these. Answer honestly.

1. What does freedom currently mean to me?

2. Do I feel free right now? Why or why not?

3. What am I waiting for before I allow myself to feel free?

4. Where in my life do I feel stuck or obligated?

5. What would change if I believed I already had enough?

AWARENESS

Where do you notice this showing up today?

☐ Waiting for a future moment to feel free
☐ Feeling stuck in responsibilities or expectations
☐ Difficulty stepping away from work or pressure
☐ Believing I need more before I can relax or enjoy life
☐ Feeling like I don't have a choice in how I spend my time
☐ Other: ____

What does that look like for you?

____
____
____
____
____
____
____
____
____
____
____
____
____
____
____

PRACTICE

When You Notice...	Try This
Waiting for freedom in the future	➤ Ask: "What is available to me right now?"
Feeling stuck or obligated	➤ Identify one small choice you can make today
Pressure to keep going	➤ Pause and give yourself permission to slow down
Believing you need more first	➤ Remind yourself: "I can choose how I show up now"

THIS WEEK

Choose one area where you want to show up differently.

This week, I will:

____
____
____
____
____
____
____
____
____
____

One moment I will practice this in:

____
____
____
____
____
____
____
____
____

What support do I need to follow through?

____
____
____
____
____
____
____
____
____

RESET

- Use this anytime you feel pressure to please or perform:
- Pause
- Take a slow breath
- Bring your attention back to yourself
- Ask: "What is true for me right now?"
- Respond from that place

WEEKLY REFLECTION

Come back to this after a few days.

What did I notice this week?

____

____

____

____

____

____

____

____

____

____

Where did I show up differently?

____

____

____

____

____

____

____

____

____

____

Where did I fall back into old patterns?

____
____
____
____
____
____
____
____
____
____
____
____

What did I learn about myself?

____
____
____
____
____
____
____
____
____
____
____
____

Where did I fall back into old patterns?

CHAPTER EIGHT

BELIEFS

SNAPSHOT

This chapter invites you to examine the beliefs you've inherited and how they shape how you think, act, and show up in your life.

- Many beliefs were formed before you had awareness or choice
- Family, culture, and systems influence what you see as true
- You may carry beliefs that no longer align with who you are
- Some beliefs create pressure, fear, or internal conflict
- Questioning beliefs can feel uncomfortable or unfamiliar
- Not all inherited beliefs are meant to be kept
- You have the ability to choose what is true for you
- Awareness allows you to separate inherited patterns from your own truth

REFLECTION

Take your time with these. Answer honestly.

1. What are some beliefs I hold about success, money, who I should be, and how I see or relate to people from different races, cultures, or backgrounds?

2. Where did these beliefs come from?

3. Which of these beliefs still feel true for me?

4. Which beliefs feel limiting, outdated, or no longer aligned?

5. What beliefs would I choose if I were starting fresh today?

AWARENESS

Where do you notice this showing up today?

☐ Acting on beliefs I've never questioned
☐ Feeling pressure to live a certain way
☐ Holding onto ideas that no longer feel true
☐ Experiencing internal conflict between what I believe and how I live
☐ Fear or discomfort when I question what I was taught
☐ Other: ____

What does that look like for you?

____
____
____
____
____
____
____
____
____
____
____
____

PRACTICE

When You Notice...	Try This
Acting from automatic beliefs	➢ Pause and ask: "Is this true for me?"
Feeling internal conflict	➢ Identify the belief underneath the feeling
Holding onto outdated ideas	➢ Ask: "Do I still choose this?"
Fear when questioning beliefs	➢ Remind yourself: "I can explore without losing myself"

THIS WEEK

Choose one area where you want to show up differently.

This week, I will:

____

____

____

____

____

____

____

____

____

One moment I will practice this in:

____

____

____

____

____

____

____

____

____

What support do I need to follow through?

____

____

____

____

____

____

____

____

RESET

- Use this anytime you feel pressure to please or perform:
- Pause
- Take a slow breath
- Bring your attention back to yourself
- Ask: "What is true for me right now?"
- Respond from that place

WEEKLY REFLECTION

Come back to this after a few days.

What did I notice this week?

____

____

____

____

____

____

____

____

____

____

____

Where did I show up differently?

____

____

____

____

____

____

____

____

____

____

____

Where did I fall back into old patterns?

____

____

____

____

____

____

____

____

____

What did I learn about myself?

____

____

____

____

____

____

____

____

Where did I fall back into old patterns?

CHAPTER NINE

FEELING

SNAPSHOT

**This chapter invites you to reconnect with your emotional world
and develop the language to understand what you feel.**

• Feelings may have been suppressed, ignored, or dismissed
• You may not have been given the words for what you feel
• Unprocessed emotions can show up as stress, anger, or
disconnection
• Avoiding feelings can become automatic
• Many men default to a limited emotional range
• Naming what you feel creates clarity and movement
• Feelings are information, not weakness
• Awareness allows you to feel without being overwhelmed or
controlled

REFLECTION

Take your time with these. Answer honestly.

1. What emotions do I feel most often?

____
____
____
____
____
____
____
____
____
____
____
____
____
____
____
____
____
____

2. Which emotions do I avoid or struggle to express?

____
____
____
____
____
____
____
____
____
____

3. When something is off, how do I usually respond?

4. What was I taught about expressing emotions growing up?

5. What would it look like to allow myself to feel more fully?

AWARENESS

Where do you notice this showing up today?

☐ Difficulty naming what I feel
☐ Defaulting to anger, silence, or withdrawal
☐ Avoiding conversations about emotions
☐ Feeling disconnected or numb
☐ Struggling to express what is really going on inside
☐ Other: ____

What does that look like for you?

____
____
____
____
____
____
____
____
____
____
____
____
____
____

PRACTICE

When You Notice...	Try This
Not knowing what you feel	➢ Pause and ask: "What am I feeling right now?"
Feeling overwhelmed	➢ Name one emotion instead of all of them
Defaulting to anger or silence	➢ Look underneath for what else is there
Avoiding emotions	➢ Stay with the feeling for a few breaths without changing it

THIS WEEK

Choose one area where you want to show up differently.

This week, I will:

____
____
____
____
____
____
____
____
____

One moment I will practice this in:

____
____
____
____
____
____
____
____
____

What support do I need to follow through?

____
____
____
____
____
____
____
____

RESET

- Use this anytime you feel pressure to please or perform:
- Pause
- Take a slow breath
- Bring your attention back to yourself
- Ask: "What is true for me right now?"
- Respond from that place

WEEKLY REFLECTION

Come back to this after a few days.

What did I notice this week?

____
____
____
____
____
____
____
____
____
____
____
____
____

Where did I stay present when I normally would not have?

____
____
____
____
____
____
____
____
____
____
____
____

Where did I fall back into old patterns?

What did I learn about how I show up in relationships?

CHAPTER TEN

WOMEN

SNAPSHOT

This chapter invites you to examine how you've been taught to see and relate to women, and how conditioning around objectification, roles, and power shapes your behavior and relationships.

- Early messages shape expectations about roles, power, and behavior
- Many men are introduced to women through objectification, not connection
- Media, culture, and peer groups normalize seeing women as bodies instead of people
- You may have learned to lead, fix, or control instead of connect
- Attraction can become entitlement, expectation, or validation
- You may judge, rank, or evaluate women without realizing it
- Emotional disconnection can show up as control, avoidance, or performance
- These patterns impact trust, intimacy, and communication
- Awareness allows you to see women as whole human beings and relate with respect and presence

REFLECTION

Take your time with these. Answer honestly.

1. What messages did I learn about women, roles, and relationships growing up?

2. When I first notice a woman, what do I focus on?

3. Where have I learned to lead, fix, or control instead of connect?

4. Have I ever judged, ranked, or objectified women without realizing it?

5. What would it look like to relate with presence, respect, and genuine curiosity?

AWARENESS

Where do you notice this showing up today?

☐ Noticing appearance before presence
☐ Judging or ranking women based on looks
☐ Trying to lead, fix, or control interactions
☐ Expecting attention, interest, or validation
☐ Difficulty connecting beyond physical attraction
☐ Consuming media that reinforces objectification
☐ Other: ____

What does that look like for you?

____
____
____
____
____
____
____
____
____
____

PRACTICE

When You Notice...	Try This
Focusing only on appearance	➢ Pause and recognize the person beyond what you see
Judging or ranking	➢ Ask: "What am I not seeing about this person?"
Wanting to lead, fix, or control	➢ Pause and listen without trying to change anything
Expecting something in return	➢ Shift to appreciation without expectation
Disconnect in interaction	➢ Stay present and listen with curiosity

THIS WEEK

Choose one area where you want to show up differently.

This week, I will:

____

____

____

____

____

____

____

____

____

One moment I will practice this in:

____

____

____

____

____

____

____

____

____

What support do I need to follow through?

____

____

____

____

____

____

____

____

RESET

- Use this anytime you feel pressure to please or perform:
- Pause
- Take a slow breath
- Bring your attention back to yourself
- Ask: "What is true for me right now?"
- Respond from that place

WEEKLY REFLECTION

Come back to this after a few days.

What did I notice this week?

____
____
____
____
____
____
____
____
____
____

Where did I stay present instead of reacting?

____
____
____
____
____
____
____
____
____
____

Where did I fall back into old patterns?

What did I learn about how I relate to women?

CHAPTER ELEVEN

AGGRESSION & VIOLENCE

SNAPSHOT

This chapter invites you to examine how aggression and violence have been normalized, modeled, and internalized, and how they show up in your life.

- Early messages often link masculinity with toughness, dominance, and control
- You may have been taught that anger is the only acceptable emotion
- Violence is normalized through media, sports, discipline, and culture
- Emotional suppression can build pressure that comes out as aggression
- Aggression is not always physical and can show up in words, tone, or silence
- You may react instead of respond when triggered
- Control can replace understanding in moments of conflict
- These patterns impact relationships, communication, and self-awareness
- Awareness allows you to respond with intention instead of reaction

REFLECTION

Take your time with these. Answer honestly.

1. What messages did I learn about anger, aggression, and being a man growing up?

____
____
____
____
____
____
____
____
____
____
____
____
____
____
____
____
____
____

2. How do I typically respond when I feel frustrated, disrespected, or out of control?

____
____
____
____
____
____
____
____
____
____

3. In what ways might aggression show up in my life (words, tone, behavior, silence)?

4. What emotions might exist underneath my anger or frustration?

5. What would it look like to respond with awareness instead of reacting automatically?

AWARENESS

Where do you notice this showing up today?

☐ Reacting quickly when triggered
☐ Raising my voice or using harsh tone
☐ Shutting down or withdrawing instead of engaging
☐ Feeling pressure build without expressing it
☐ Using control instead of communication
☐ Difficulty identifying emotions beyond anger
☐ Other: ____

What does that look like for you?

____
____
____
____
____
____
____
____
____
____
____
____

PRACTICE

When You Notice...	Try This
Feeling triggered or reactive	➤ Pause before responding
Anger rising	➤ Take a slow breath and feel it in your body
Wanting to control or dominate	➤ Ask: "What am I actually feeling?"
Shutting down or withdrawing	➤ Name one honest feeling
Escalating tension	➤ Slow down your words and tone

THIS WEEK

Choose one area where you want to show up differently.

This week, I will:

____
____
____
____
____
____
____
____
____

One moment I will practice this in:

____
____
____
____
____
____
____
____
____

What support do I need to follow through?

____
____
____
____
____
____
____
____

RESET

- Use this anytime you feel pressure to please or perform:
- Pause
- Take a slow breath
- Bring your attention back to yourself
- Ask: "What is true for me right now?"
- Respond from that place

WEEKLY REFLECTION

Come back to this after a few days.

What did I notice this week?

Where did I pause instead of reacting?

Where did I fall back into old patterns?

What did I learn about how I handle anger or conflict?

Where did I fall back into old patterns?

CHAPTER TWELVE

THE PATH FORWARD

SNAPSHOT

This chapter invites you to redefine success from the inside out and choose a way of living that feels authentic, aligned, and fully present.

- Success shifts from performance to alignment
- Being healed, whole, and present becomes the foundation
- Your worth is no longer tied to achievement or approval
- You begin to live from your values instead of expectations
- Love, Joy, Service, and Play become guiding principles
- You show up as your authentic self, not a version you think you need to be
- Relationships, presence, and meaning take priority
- Success becomes something you experience, not something you chase
- Awareness allows you to live a life that feels like your own

REFLECTION

Take your time with these. Answer honestly.

1. What does success mean to me now?

2. Where in my life do I feel most aligned and authentic?

3. Where am I still performing, proving, or seeking approval?

4. What does being healed, whole, and present look like in my daily life?

5. How can I bring more Love, Joy, Service, and Play into my life right now?

AWARENESS

Where do you notice this showing up today?

☐ Living in alignment with my values
☐ Feeling present and engaged in my life
☐ Letting go of the need to prove or perform
☐ Making space for joy, connection, and rest
☐ Showing up as my authentic self
☐ Noticing when I slip back into old patterns
☐ Other: ____

What does that look like for you?

____
____
____
____
____
____
____
____
____
____

PRACTICE

When You Notice...	**Try This**
Feeling pressure to perform or prove	➤ Pause and ask: "What feels true for me?"
Disconnection or misalignment	➤ Bring your attention back to your body and breath
Old patterns returning	➤ Gently acknowledge it and choose again
Forgetting what matters	➤ Reconnect with Love, Joy, Service, and Play
Rushing through life	➤ Slow down and be present in the moment

THIS WEEK

Choose one area where you want to show up differently.

This week, I will:

____
____
____
____
____
____
____
____
____

One moment I will practice this in:

____
____
____
____
____
____
____
____
____
____

What support do I need to follow through?

____
____
____
____
____
____
____
____

RESET

- Use this anytime you feel pressure to please or perform:
- Pause
- Take a slow breath
- Bring your attention back to yourself
- Ask: "What is true for me right now?"
- Respond from that place

WEEKLY REFLECTION

Come back to this after a few days.

What did I notice this week?

____
____
____
____
____
____
____
____
____
____

Where did I choose differently?

____
____
____
____
____
____
____
____
____
____

Where did I return to old patterns?

What did I learn about how I want to live moving forward?

MUSIC COMPANION

Music is part of this work.

Some experiences are easier to feel than explain. The songs referenced throughout the book are meant to support reflection, awareness, and connection in a way that words alone cannot.

Use these playlists in whatever way supports you. You may listen during reflection, while walking, driving, or anytime you want to reconnect with yourself and what you are working through.

ACCESS THE PLAYLISTS

SPOTIFY

APPLE MUSIC

LIVING THIS FORWARD

You do not need to get this perfect. What matters is your willingness to stay with it, to notice what is happening, to be honest about your experience, and to return when you lose your way.

There will be moments when this feels clear and moments when it does not. That is part of the process. Progress does not come from forcing change, but from staying present long enough to see what is true and choosing how you want to respond.

This is not about doing more or becoming someone different. It is about how you live, one moment at a time, through your attention, your honesty, and your choices.

Stay present, tell yourself the truth, and take the next honest step. Over time, that consistency changes how you respond, how you relate, and how you experience your life.

www.ingramcontent.com/pod-product-compliance
Lightning Source LLC
Chambersburg PA
CBHW081223130726
47997CB00009B/2760